www.ReclaimJoy.com

Miracles

Tracy's Favorite Quotations about Miracles

Compiled by
Tracy Brown, RScP

- www.ReclaimJoy.com -

About Tracy Brown

Tracy Brown is an author, speaker and popular teacher and retreat leader throughout the New Thought Movement. Based in Dallas, Texas, she is actively involved as a teacher and leader at CSLDallas.

She is the host of "Poetry, Prayer and Practice" on the New Thought Media Network, where she is also part of the team that produces the Saturday Science of Mind Conversation Series. As a licensed spiritual coach, she maintains an active coaching practice focused on helping her clients integrate their mental, physical, financial and spiritual priorities.

Tracy served for six years on the international governing Board for Centers for Spiritual Living (CSL), including three years as Chair of that Board. Within CSL she is also a recipient of The Ernest Holmes Award and an honorary doctorate degree.

For More Information:
www.ReclaimJoy.com
www.ITurnToPrayer.com
www.StainedGlassSpirit.net

f t in

1

"Miracles are not contrary to nature, but only contrary to what we know about nature."

Saint Augustine

2

"All the works of Nature are Miracles, and nothing makes them appear otherwise but our familiarity with them."

Samuel Butler

3

"To contrast the size of the oak with that of the parent acorn, as if the poor seed had paid all costs from its slender strongbox, may serve for a child's wonder. But the real miracle lies in that divine league which bound all the forces of nature to the service of the tiny germ in fulfilling its destiny."

James Russell Lowell

4

"Don't gasp at a miracle that is truly miraculous
because the magic lies in the fact that you knew it was
there for you all along."

Toni Morrison

5

"Because we fail to realize that Principle is not bound by precedent, we limit our faith to that which has already been accomplished, and few 'miracles' result. When, through intuition, faith finds its proper place under Divine Law, there are no limitations and what are called miraculous results follow."

Ernest Holmes

6

"Miracles, in the sense of phenomena we cannot explain, surround us on every hand: life itself is the miracle of miracles."

George Bernard Shaw

7

"Miracles arise from our ignorance of nature, not from nature."

Montaigne

8

"Every time God's children have thrown away fear in
pursuit of honesty – trying to communicate
themselves, understood or not – miracles have
happened."

Duke Ellington

9

"Miracles do not, in fact, break the laws of nature."

C.S. Lewis

f t in

10

As my mind can conceive of more good, the barriers and blocks dissolve. My life becomes full of little miracles popping up out of the blue.

Louise L. Hay

11

"Miracles are like pimples, because once you start looking for them you find more than you ever dreamed you'd see."

Lemony Snicket

f t in

12

"True miracles are created by men when they use the courage and intelligence that God gave them."

Jean Anouilh

13

"This is the first miracle: a man becomes his dreams.
Then it is that the line between what he does and is
and his dream melts away."

Howard Thurman

14

"All the things of the universe are perfect miracles,
each as profound as any."

Walt Whitman

15

"A miracle is a series of natural events, occurring in the right sequence and at the right time, to produce wonderful events."

Michael Rann & Elizabeth Arrott

16

"Expect a miracle!"

Oral Roberts

17

"I choose to live my life as if it is a miracle unfolding.
What about you? "

Tracy Brown

18

"To the average person, when a result is obtained by this method of work [prayer treatment], it looks as though a miracle has happened, but such is not the case. It is only a miracle as everything else in life is a miracle. A definite, conscious idea has been set in motion in the Subjective World, which accepts ideas at their own valuation and tends to act upon them."

Ernest Holmes

19

"We are miracles. Each of us is an absolute astonishment. So whether you believe in miracles or not, we still are. We still partake of 'miracledom.'"

Ruby Doe

20

"Men talk about Bible miracles because there no miracle in their lives. Cease to gnaw that crust. There is ripe fruit over your head."

Henry David Thoreau

21

"The invariable mark of wisdom is to see the miraculous in the common.“

Ralph Waldo Emerson

22

"Where there is great love there are always miracles."

Willa Cather

23

"The dream was always running ahead of me. To catch up, to live for a moment in unison with it, that was the miracle. "

Anais Nin

24

"The miracle is not to fly in the air, or to walk on the water; but to walk on the earth."

Thích Nhất Hạnh

25

"Mysteries are not necessarily miracles."

Johann Wolfgang von Goethe

f   t   in

Your Next Best You

Coaching by Tracy Brown, RScP

If you are ready to integrate your mental, emotional, physical, financial and spiritual priorities, you are ready for coaching with Tracy Brown, RScP.

- The primary difference between spirituality-based coaching and psychotherapy is we spend very little time analyzing the past and a lot of time identifying how you want to live now to achieve what you want to have or who you want to be.

- The primary difference between spirituality-based coaching and mainstream life coaching is we are intentional about integrating spiritual values and priorities with your personal, professional and financial priorities or goals.

For more information visit:

www.ReclaimJoy.com or www.TracyBrownRScP.com